Making Out

in

Revised Edition

by John Clewley
revised by Benjawan Jai-Ua and
Michael Golding

TUTTLE PUBLISHING
Boston • Rutland, Vermont • Tokyo

Published by Tuttle Publishing, an imprint of Periplus Editions (HK) Ltd
with editorial offices at 153 Milk Street, Boston Massachussetts 02109
and 130 Joo Seng Road, #06-01/03 Singapore 368357.

LCC Card No. 94-60443   *495.918*
ISBN 0-8048-3555-1

Printed in Singapore

Distributed by:

Japan
Tuttle Publishing
Yaekari Building 3F
5-4-12 Osaki, Shinagawa-ku
Tokyo 1410032
Japan
Tel: (03) 5437 0171
Fax: (03) 5437 0755
Email: tuttle-sales@gol.com

North America, Latin America & Europe
Tuttle Publishing
364 Innovation Drive
North Clarendon, VT 05759-9436, USA
Tel: (802) 773 8930
Fax: (802) 773 6993
Email: info@tuttlepublishing.com
www.tuttlepublishing.com

Asia Pacific
Berkeley Books Pte Ltd
130 Joo Seng Road, 06-01/03
Singapore 368357
Tel: (65) 6280 1330
Fax: (65) 6280 6290
Email: inquiries@periplus.com.sg

08 07 06 05 04
6 5 4 3 2 1

Contents

Introduction

So you want to speak ***phaasǎa thammadaa*** *(phaasǎa thammadaa)* or **common Thai** like the Thais do, but you're scared of the five tones, the funny script, and the fact that you didn't do so well in high school French. You may have tried different Thai language learning books, but you just can't deal with all the funny-looking tone systems, the funky grammar and the far-out rules. And then what the books tell you seems far from what you hear when you're with Thais in the office or at bars. They seem to use phrases that somehow didn't find their way into those Thai language grammar-based textbooks!

You're frustrated; you want to meet Thais and say some authentic Thai while you're at it. Well, forget your worries and let this little book serve as your guide to the back streets and secret passageways of the language! Don't worry too much about the tones, they'll come with practice. And while you're about it, there's a barrowful of help here too so that you don't say **suay** "bad luck" instead of **sǔay** "pretty"!

If you just want to talk to Thais on a day-to-day basis, you're going to have to break out of that strict grammar mould. You're going to listen more, become receptive to language and be more aware of the earthier currents in your communication. We all know what benefits you'll gain from following these true and tried tips. This book will guide you in your quest, and give you a taste of Thai tones too. So read on...

INFORMATION

As you see from the difference between **suay** and **sŭay**, Thai is a tonal language. It has five tones: mid or level, low, falling, high and rising—this is the order the Thais use. While the tone on an individual word can be vitally important, in general context, tones are not something to worry about. You can give the context by carefully noting then pronouncing the phrases in this book. The section on pronunciation tips will help you do this. As for the tones, you'll learn those next, but try to find a Thai friend who has a few hours free first.

Now the good news. You can forget general verb tenses and the complicated grammar of European languages. Past tenses are replaced with time words, often given at the start or finish of the phrase, while future is simple: add *ca* before the verb to mean "will." Thai also has a relatively simple grammar that's similar to English: subject, verb, and object/predicate. But note that an adjective follows the noun it describes (**khon sŭay** means a **beautiful** person)—this isn't hard when you use the phrases given here.

There's also no need to bother with "a" and "the" as you don't really need them in Thai. Thais will often omit subjects such as "I" or "you" and just use a verb and an object—where this is the case, we have shown the words that can be omitted in parentheses ( ).

You will hear Thais using **khráp** and **khâ/khá** at the end of sentences (as well as several other words!) These are called polite particles that will help you if you get used to using them all the time. They can be used with nearly every sentence in this book, so use them often. If you do, Thais will see you as a person with manners, even speaking the everyday language here—and yes, it does sound like "crap" but you want to get (it) on with Thais don't you? Males use **khráp**, and females **khâ** at the end of statements, and *khráp* and *khá* after questions. You'll see men have it easy! In this book, male words are shown with ♂ and female ones with ♀ when necessary, although most of the time the particles are left out to save space. Just add them when you can.

Here are a couple of examples:

(khun) Ca pai nǎi khráp ♂?
[male to female]

Where are you going?

(chán ♀) Ca pai súeh khǎwng khâ ♀
[female to male]

I'm going shopping.

khráp ♂/khá ♀ is the easiest way to say "yes" in reply to the question:

Ca pai dûai mái (khráp ♂/khá ♀)
khráp?/khâ?

Wanna go too?
Sure.

Another word that varies according to gender is the first-person pronoun (I or me). Men use *phǒm ♂* and women *chán ♀* or, more nicely, *dichán ♀*.

TONE TIPS

As you've seen, Thai has five tones: mid, low, falling, high and rising. In this book we've used a simple but general system to show them as marks above the words. Have another look at the examples above in INFORMATION to get an idea. Let's use an example—if we take the word *maa* (to come), the tones would be written as:

mid—*maa* (the level or plain tone—no mark)
low—*màa* (the mark points low: ↘)
falling—*mâa* (the mark shows you throwing a stone over a cliff ↘)
high—*máa* (the mark points high: ↗)
rising—*mǎa* (the mark shows you scooping water out of a well ↗)

Ask a Thai friend to give you some "tone practice." Be careful if you can, because **máa maa** means a horse is coming, but **măa maa** means a dog is coming (and Thais think dogs are low life!) Still, in context you won't have too many problems.

PRONUNCIATION TIPS

Vowels

The five main vowels: *aa, eh, ii, oh* and *uu* are pronounced as in Spanish, Italian and several other European languages as follows (you can get a better idea of some short vowels by saying the longer ones first, then shortening the sound):

a as in **after**;	*aa* as in **father**
e as in t**r**ead;	*eh* as in t**r**ade
i as in b**it**;	*ii* as in b**eat**
o as in b**oat**;	*oh* as in b**eau**
u as in **rule**;	*uu* as in **rue/roo**

The other four pure vowels of Thai are written with two letters as, apart from **y**, English only has "five written vowels." In Thai these additional vowels are *ueh, aeh, aw* and *oeh*. Now's the time to coax a Thai friend into saying these vowels which are / ˝ /,/ɯ/,/ɔ/, and /ɤˆ/ in Thai. Here are some *close* examples, note the first is said with the teeth clenched together at first:

ue as in **oeuf**;	*ueh* as in **eu**gh... [that's awful]
ae as in h**ea**d;	*aeh* as in h**ai**r
aw as in h**o**nk;	*aw* as in h**awthor**ne [but no "r" sound]
oe as in m**o**ther [no "r"];	*oeh* as in h**e**r [no "r"]

Other Thai vowels are just mixtures of these. Here are some examples:

ai as in **eye** si**gh**t; *ai* as in si**gh**
awi as in b**oy**
oi as in sh**owy**
oei like joey, but change to j**er-y** [no 'r']
ia as in id**ea**
uai as in going **too–eh?**
ua as in t**our** (too–uh)
uea as in **eu**gh with the jaw dropping to say "*a*" after
ueai as above with an "**eh**" added(*!*)
aeo as in **ai**r [no "r"] with an "**oh**" added at the end
eo as in m**ayo**
iao as in Tok**yo**

Consonants

Many Thai consonants are pronounced as written, but there are some which are marked with an "h" after to show there's air required to make them. Say *tie* out loud, now "Thailand"; *pooh get*, the sound of "Phuket." Two are said between English sounds: a Thai *p* is close to that in "speed"; the *t* to that in "stopped", and *k* to that in skill (like a "g"). With a "h" added, the Thai *ph* is like that in **p**ie, *th* like that in "tea," and *kh* as in "**k**ind." Now these all match the Thai Government system, believe it or not.

Make a Thai *t* by pushing the tongue behind the front teeth, then releasing it to make the consonant between *th* and *d*. Make a *p* by pushing the lips together then releasing them to make the sound between *ph* and *b*.

One consonant that needs some practice is the *ng* at the start of words(*!*). Start with saying "singing" over and over, then make it "sing–ing," then "si–nging," then finally "nging" by itself. It takes time—work at it without sound if you can!

The Thai *j* is more like *tch*; it's written as **c** to match the latest UN convention. As an example, the word for "China" or "Chinese" is *ciin*, pronounced like the English "Jean". Good, you've got it!

The consonants *d, b, l, r, m, n, w, y, f, s, ch* and *h,* are easy ... they're just the same as you're used to.

The imitated pronunciation used throughout the book is the closest English equivalent to a speech sound in Thai.

THAIGLISH

Apart from the tonal nature of the Thai language, there are other significant differences between Thai and English. You **can** use English with Thais, especially in major cities like Bangkok and Chiang Mai, but you must be aware of how they pronounce English words. For example, a Thai might say "Have a *nai* day" or "Do you want some *ai?*" (ice!) Since Thai lacks a final "s" sound, Thais neither hear nor produce it. Bear this in mind when you use any English, and try to keep things simple—try to **Thai-ify** the English words so you'll be better understood!

Similarly, if you ask someone if they have something—a shopkeeper, for example—he/she may well answer "no haf," which is a direct translation of the Thai *mâi mii* (rhymes with 'why me'!). Most Thais know a little English, but they often use it "through" their own language, giving rise to words that are part English and part Thai—words that might be referred to as "Thaiglish." Still, an understanding of this can help you communicate better.

Like many Asian languages, Thai is incorporating and adopting more English words than ever before—this is especially so in the scientific and business community. It is also cool for young Thais, especially in Bangkok, to include English words in their everyday speech. The word-borrowing is known in Thai as ***tháp sàp*** (laying language on top). One example of this from Bangkok, is the word ***wôeh*** pronounced like "were" with a falling tone. It comes from "over," meaning "over-priced" and is easier to say than ***phaeh ng koehn pay.***

And another example:

An ni chái dâi rúe plào?	**Can I use this (does it work)?**
Man mâi wóehk.	**It doesn't work.**

Here are some common words and how they sound in Thai (hyphens are used here to better identify the syllables):

Apartment	*a-pháat-mént*
Bank	*báeng*
Bar	*bah*
Battery	*bát-toe-rîi*
Care/Don't care	*khae/mâi khae*
Classic	*khláa-sik*
Computer	*khawm-phiu-tôeh*
Copy	*kháwp-pîi*
Coupon	*khuu-pong*
Disco	*dis-khôh*
Doughnut	*doh-nát*
Fashion	*fae-chân*
Free	*frii*
Football	*fút-bawn*
Hotel	*hoh-tên*
Ice-cream	*ai-tiim*
Jam	*yaem*
Nice	*nái*
Pizza	*phít-sâa*
Romantic	*roh-maen-tic*
Sandwich	*saen-wít*
Serious	*sii-rîat*

Shock	*cháwk*
Shopping	*cháwp-pîng*
Sexy	*sáek-sǐi*
Six	*sik*
Smart	*sa-máat*
Spaghetti	*sa-paa-két-tîi*
Stamp	*sa-taem*
Steak	*sa-téh*
Sure	*chua*
Technology	*the-k-noh-loh-yîi*
TV	*thii-wii*
Video	*wi-dii-oh*
View	*wiu*

CULTURAL NOTES

If you're going to get along using Thai in Thailand, you should be aware of several key concepts at the heart of Thai culture. First there's the notion of **sanùk**, or fun. Thais are fun-loving people: they like to laugh, tell jokes, and play. If you make a mistake when trying your Thai language skills (say you make a mistake ordering a kilo of penises (**khuay**) instead of a kilo of bananas (**kûay**) at the local market, then laugh and enjoy the joke. More often than not, the Thais will be laughing with you, not at you. Laughing and smiling at your mistakes will endear you to the locals and give you a reputation of one who likes **sanùk**. And Thai people genuinely do **ápichêht** (appreciate) anyone who makes an effort to speak their language.

Another key concept is **thîao** (tio with a falling tone), or "going out." Thais love to **thîao**, whether it means going to the movies, taking a walk, or indulging in one of the national pastimes: eating. Join in the fun and tag along. However, do remember as a westerner (**faràng**), you might be expected to pay—but prices **are** generally cheap.

Perhaps the most famous phrase, and a concept of Thai culture, is ***mâi pen rai***, which means "never mind." This carries meanings of "don't worry," "don't get hung up on things" and "it's OK." The phrase is useful in confrontations when you need to back down. Thais do not generally want confrontation—they don't want to "lose face" either, but neither do they want **you** to!—and will do their utmost to keep things "cool." They prefer people who are ***cai yen*** (**c** is read like a *j*, remember—stay cool) to those who display anger in public: **be** cool and you'll do okay.

So, don't worry; take your problems lightly, and go out there and have fun—***thiao hâi sanùk***! In no time at all you'll understand why Thailand is called the "Land of smiles."

chôhk dii ná—Good luck!

What's Up? 1

What's up?
  (What's going on?)

เป็นยังไง
Pen yang ngai?

How's it going?

เป็นยังไงบ้าง
Pen yang ngai bâang?

Adding the **bâang** to **pen yang ngai** is like adding "tell me all about it"

How are you?

สบายดีหรือ
Sabaay dii lǒeh?

What's happening?

เป็นไง
Pen ngai?

This is a shorter form of **yang ngai** and is, no doubt, easier to say!

What have you been doing?

ตอนนี้ทำอะไร
Tawn níi tham arai?

What have you been talking about?

กำลังคุยเรื่องอะไร
Kamlang khui rûeang arai?

Haven't seen you around here for a while, have I?

ไม่ได้เจอนานแล้วนะ
Mây dây coeh naan láeo na?

Ná is a particle that adds an informal feel to what you're saying. It kind of says "isn't it?" "don't you?" "have you?", and asks for agreement from the other person. Here it's like adding "have I?"

Is (Suphatra/Lek) OK?

(สุพัตรา/เล็ก) สบายดีหรือ
(Suphátraa/lék)
sabaay dii lŏeh?

How's (Suphatra/Lek) doing?

(สุพัตรา/เล็ก) เป็นยังไง
(Suphátraa/lék)
pen yang ngai?

Your guy/girl will have a given Thai name as well as a nickname. Once you know their name, or better still, their nickname, try to mimic it exactly, if you can. Use it for "you" as happens here.

Fifty-fifty.

ห้าสิบ ห้าสิบ
Hâa sìp hâa sìp.

So so.

เรื่อย ๆ
Rûeai rûeai.
งั้น ๆ
Ngán ngán.

I'm fine.

สบายดี
Sabaay dii.

Are you doing anything?

ทำอะไรหรือเปล่า
Tham arai rúe plào?

Nothing much.

ไม่ได้ทำ
Mây dây tham.

Nothing special.

ไม่มีอะไรพิเศษ
Mây mii arai phísèht.

I was just thinking.

กำลังคิดอยู่
Kamlang khít yùu.

I was just daydreaming ...

กำลังฝันว่า ...
Kamlang făn wâa

Leave me alone!	อย่ามายุ่ง Yàa maa yûng!
Don't annoy me!	อย่ายุ่ง Yàa yûng!
It's none of your business!	ธุระไม่ใช่ Thurá mâi châi!

By adding an inquisitive tone to the following words or phrases you can turn them into a question or a request for affirmation:

Really?	หรือ Lŏeh?

Spelt **rŭe** in Thai, this is usually pronounced as **lŏeh**. Thais regularly swap **r** and **l**, and the vowel *oeh* is easier to say than *ueh*!

Is that so?	จริงหรือ Cing lŏeh?
Is that right?	ใช่ไหม Châi mái?
How come?	ได้ยังไง Dâi yang ngai?
Why?	ทำไม Thammai?

What do you mean?

หมายความว่ายังไง
Măi khwaam wâa yang
    ngai?

Is something wrong?

เป็นอะไรไป
Pen arai pai?

Is there a problem?

มีปัญหาหรือ
Mii panhăa lŏeh?

What's the difference?

ต่างกันยังไง
Tàang kan yang ngai?

What?

อะไร
Arai?

You may hear your Thai friends say the very informal *arai wá* amongst
themselves or when arguing. They will discourage you from using the *wá*
particle, as it might get you into hot water if used inappropriately!

What? (informal)

อะไรนะ
Arai ná?

Why not?

ทำไมล่ะ
Thammai lâ?

Why not ...?

ทำไมไม่ ...
Thammai mâi ...?

Are you serious?

พูดจริงหรือ
Phûut cing lŏeh?

Are you sure?

แน่ใจหรือ
Nâeh cai lŏeh?

**You don't mean it,
do you?**

ไม่ได้พูดจริง ๆ ใช่ไหม
Mâi dâi phûut cing
cing, châi mái?

Literally means "You're telling me tales, aren't you?"

You're joking!

พูดเล่นมั้ง
Phûut lên máng!

You're joking, aren't you?

พูดเล่นใช่ไหม
Phûut lên châi mái?

That's right!

ใช่แล้ว
Châi láehw!

Absolutely!

แน่นอน
Nâeh nawn!

Definitely!

แหง ๆ
Ngăeh ngăeh!

Of course!

ชัว
Chua!

Derived from the English "sure!"

You better believe it!

ต้องเชื่อเลย
Tâwng chûea loei!

That's it!	นั่นแหละ Nân làe!
I guess so.	คิดว่ายังงั้น Khít wâa yang ngán.
It might be true.	อาจจะจริง Àat ca cing.
Maybe.	อาจจะ Àat ca.
Maybe not.	อาจจะไม่ Àat ca mâi.
I doubt it.	สงสัย Sŏng săi.
I wonder.	ไม่แน่ Mâi nâeh.
I bet.	ฉันว่า Chán wâa.
I don't think so.	ไม่เห็นด้วย Mâi hěn dûai.

Literally means "I don't agree with that."

I'm not sure.	ไม่แน่ Mâi nâeh.
There's no way to know.	ไม่มีทางรู้ Mâi mii thaang rúu.
I can't say for sure. (I don't know.)	ไม่รู้ Mâi rúu.
You're kidding me!	ล้อเล่นใช่ไหม Láw lên châi mái?
This is too good to be true!	ดีเกินไป Dii koehn pai!
No way!	ไม่มีทาง Mâi mii thaang!
Stop joking!	อย่าพูดเล่น· Yàa phûut lên!
That's not right!	ไม่ใช่ Mâi châi!
That's impossible!	เป็นไปไม่ได้ Pen pai mâi dâi!
Forget it!	ช่างมัน Châang man!

I've had enough!   พอแล้ว
                           Phaw láeo!

Bullshit!   โกหก
                           Kohhòk!

Literally means "You lie."

I don't care.   ไม่สน, ไม่แคร์
                           Mâi sŏn, mâi khae.

It means nothing to me. ไม่มีความหมาย
                           Mâi mii khwaam măi.

I'm not interested.   ไม่สนใจ
                           Mâi sŏncai.

I think so too.   ฉันก็ว่ายังงั้นแหละ
                           Chán kâw wâa
                             yang ngán làe.

So am I.   ฉันด้วย
                           Chán dûai.

I see. (I get it.)

รู้แล้ว
Rúu láeo.

All right, I understand.

เอาเถอะ เข้าใจแล้ว
Ao thòe khâwcai láeo.

All right, no problem.

เอาเถอะ ไม่มีปัญหา
Ao thòe mâi mii panhǎa.

That was good.

ดีนี่
Dii nîi.

Right on!

ถูกเป๊ง
Thùuk pěng!

Great!

เยี่ยม
Yîam!

No problem!

ไม่มีปัญหา
Mâi mii panhǎa!

I did it!

ฉันทำ
Chán tham!

Because ...

เพราะ ...
Phráw ...

But ...

แต่ ...
Tàe

Got a Minute?

Got a minute?

ว่างไหม
Wâang mái?

Literally means "Are you free?"

'Til when?

ถึงเมื่อไหร่
Thŭeng mûearài?

About when?

ราวกี่โมง
Rao kìi mohng?

Literally means "About what o'clock?"

About what time?

ประมาณกี่โมง
Pramaan kìi mohng?

Is it too early?

เร็วไปไหม
Reo pai mái?

Is it too late?

ช้าไปไหม
Cháa pai mái?

When is it convenient for you?

สะดวกเมื่อไหร่
Sadùak mûearài?

| How about the eighteenth? | สิบแปดได้ไหม |
| | Sìp pàeht dâi mái? |

| Then when can you make it? | มาได้กี่โมง |
| | Maa dâi kìi mohng? |

| What time can I come over? | ให้มาหากี่โมง |
| | Hâi maa hăa kìi mohng? |

| When can I see you? | จะได้เจออีกเมื่อไหร่ |
| | Ca dâi coeh ìik mûearài? |

| What time do we leave? | จะไปเมื่อไหร่ |
| | Ca pai mûearài? |

| What time do we arrive? | จะถึงเมื่อไหร่ |
| | Ca thŭeng mûearài? |

| Are you ready? | พร้อมไหม |
| | Phráwm mái? |

| When can you do it? | จะทำตอนไหน |
| | Ca tham tawn năi? |

| When can you be there? | จะไปที่นั่นกี่โมง |
| | Ca pai thîi nân kìi mohng? |

How long will it take? จะนานเท่าไหร่
Ca naan thâorài?

Maybe later. อาจจะทีหลัง
Àat ca thii lăng.

Not yet. ยัง
Yang.

Not now. (Wait a little.) ไม่ใช่ตอนนี้
Mâi châi tawn níi.

Last time ... ครั้งที่แล้ว
Khráng thîi láeo

I don't know when. ไม่รู้เมื่อไหร่
Mâi rúu mûearài.

I don't know now/yet. ยังไม่รู้
Yang mâi rúu.

Sometime(s). บางที
Baang thii.

Someday บางวัน
Baang wan

Soon

เร็ว ๆ นี้
Reo reo níi

Next life

ชาติหน้า
Châat nâa

Said as a joke, although there may be some truth to it!

Anytime is fine.

เมื่อไหร่ก็ได้
Mûearài kâw dâai.

Always

เสมอ
Samŏeh.

You decide when.

บอกมาว่าเมื่อไหร่
Bàwk maa wâa mûearài.

That's a bad day for me.

วันนั้นไม่ดี
Wan nán mâi dii.

How about Tuesday?

วันอังคารล่ะ
Wan angkhaan lâ?

That day is fine.

วันนั้นก็ได้
Wan nán kâw dâi.

Let's begin!

เริ่มเถอะ
Rôehm thòe!

It won't take a minute.

ไม่นาน
Mâi naan.

Let's continue.

ทำต่อเถอะ
Tham tàw thòe.

Do it later.

เอาไว้ก่อน
Ao wái kàwn.

I'll finish soon.

เดี๋ยวเสร็จ
Dĭao sèt.

"Finished" in Thai means completed, and may be used during lovemaking.

I finished.

เสร็จแล้ว
Sèt láeo.

Finished?

เสร็จแล้วหรือ
Sèt láeo lŏeh?

Finished already?

เรียบร้อยแล้วหรือ
Rîap ráwi láeo lŏeh?

Say What? 3

Listen

ฟังนะ
Fang ná.

Listen (before you do anything else).

ฟังก่อน
Fang kàwn.

Listen to me.

ฟังฉัน
Fang chán.

Don't listen (no need to listen).

ไม่ต้องฟัง
Mâi tâwng fang.

Don't ask (me like that).

อย่าถาม (ยังงั้น)
Yàa thăam.

Did you hear me?

ได้ยินไหม
Dâiyin mái?

I couldn't hear.

ฟังไม่ได้ยิน
Fang mâi dâiyin.

I didn't hear.

ไม่ได้ยิน
Mâi dâiyin.

I don't want to hear.

ไม่อยากฟัง
Mâi yàak fang.

Say something.

พูดซิ
Phûut sí.

What are you talking about?

พูดเรื่องอะไร
Phûut rûeang arai?

**You shouldn't say
   things like that.**

ไม่ควรพูดยังงั้น
Mâi khuan phûut
   yang ngán.

You said that, didn't you?

คุณพูดใช่ไหม
Khun phûut, châi mái?

I didn't say anything.

ไม่ได้พูดซะหน่อย
Mâi dâi phûut sá nàwi.

Let's speak Thai.

พูดไทยกัน
Phûut thai kan.

Let's continue to talk.

คุยกันต่อ
Khui kan tàw.

Let's talk about it later.

พูดเรื่องนั้นทีหลัง
Phûut rûeang nán thii
   lăng.

I don't want to talk.

ไม่อยากพูด
Mâi yàak phûut.

**I don't want to talk
   about it.**

ไม่อยากพูดเรื่องนั้น
Mâi yàak phûut
   rûeang nán.

No need to excuse yourself.

ไม่ต้องขอโทษ
Mâi tâwng khǎw thôht.

Literally means "No need to ask for punishment."

Don't make excuses.

ไม่ต้องแก้ตัว
Mâi tâwng kâeh tua.

That's not a good excuse.

ไม่ใช่ข้อแก้ตัวที่ดี
Mâi châi khâw
    kâeh tua thîi dii.

Stop complaining!
   (Stop whining!)

หยุดบ่นซะที
Yùt bòn sá thii!

Do you know what you're saying?

พูดอะไรออกมา
Phûut arai àwk maa?

Don't talk so loudly.

อย่าพูดเสียงดัง
Yàa phûut sǐang dang.

Speak up.

พูดดัง ๆ
Phûut dang dang.

Speak more slowly.

พูดช้า ๆ หน่อย
Phûut chá cháa nàwi.

You can double adverbs (like slowly) to show your own thoughts.
When doubled, the first one is often shortened as here: *chá cháa*

Say (it) again?

พูดอีกทีซิ
Phûut ìik thii sí?

Could you say it again?

พูดอีกทีได้ไหม
Phûut ìik thii dâi mái?

There was another noise.

มีเสียงแทรก
Mii sǐang sâehk.

I didn't hear you.

ไม่ได้ยิน
Mâi dâiyin.

What was that?

นั่นอะไร
Nân arai?

Did you say something?

คุณพูดอะไรรึเปล่า
Khun phûut arai rúe plào?

I missed that. (I didn't catch what you said.)

คุณว่าอะไรนะ
Khun wâa arai ná.

Sorry, I missed that.

โทษที อะไรนะ
Thôht thii, arai ná.

You mumbled.

คุณพูดพึมพำ
Khun phûutphuem pham.

You sighed.

คุณถอนใจ
Khun thǎwn cai.

You moaned/groaned.

คุณคราง
Khun khraang.

You shouted.

คุณตะโกน
Khun takohn.

I farted.

ดิฉัน/ผมตด
Dichán ♀/phǒm ♂ tòt.

Did You See That?

Look!

ดูซิ
Duu si!

Look at that!

ดูนั่น
Duu nân!

Don't look!

อย่าดู
Yàa duu!

Did you see (it)?

เห็นไหม
Hěn mái?

I saw (it).

เห็น
Hěn.

I didn't see (it).

ไม่เห็น
Mâi hěn.

I couldn't see (it).	มองไม่เห็น Mawng mâi hĕn.
Do you want to see (it)?	อยากดูไหม Yàak duu mái?
I don't want to see (it).	ไม่อยากดู Mâi yàak duu.
Seen Somchai/Pet ?	เห็นสมชาย/เป็ดไหม Hĕn sŏmchai/pèt mái?

All Thai nicknames, like Thai names, have a meaning. This one means "duck." Like some Western names (eg Fanny, Dick), they might sound funny, but are not laughed at.

I want to see you soon.	อยากเจอเร็ว ๆ Yàak coeh reo reo.
I saw Dao.	เห็นดาว Hĕn dao.

Being a proper name, **Dao** also means "star" or "planet."

I met Dao.	เจอดาว Coeh dao.
So we've met again, eh?	เจอกันอีกแล้วหรือ Coeh kan ìik láeo lŏeh?

I wanted to see you.　　อยากเจอคุณ
　　　　　　　　　　　　Yàak coeh khun.

I missed you.　　　　คิดถึง
　　　　　　　　　　　　Khít thŭeng.

I'll show you.　　　　จะทำให้ดู
　　　　　　　　　　　　Ca tham hâi duu.

I don't want to show you.　ไม่อยากทำให้ดู
　　　　　　　　　　　　Mâi yàak tham hâi duu.

I won't show you.　　　ไม่ทำให้ดู
　　　　　　　　　　　　Mâi tham hâi duu.

Let's Go! 5

Come here.
มานี่
Maa nîi.

Come over here.
มาทางนี่
Maa thaang nîi.

Come later.
เดี๋ยวมา
Dǐaw maa.

Come again.
มาอีกนะ
Maa iik ná.

Can you come?
มาได้ไหม
Maa dâi mái?

Won't you come along?
ไม่มาหรือ
Mâi maa lǒeh?

It is written as **rǔeh**, but generally pronounced **lǒeh**.

Won't you come with us?
ไม่มากับเราหรือ
Mâi maa kàp rao lǒeh?

Won't you come with me?
ไม่มากับฉันหรือ
Mâi maa kàp chán lǒeh?

She is coming here.
เขากำลังมานี่
Kháo kamlang maa nîi.

I'm coming; wait a second.
กำลังมา รอเดี๋ยว
Kamlang maa, raw dǐao.

| **I can go.** | ไปได้ |
| | Pai dâi. |

| **I think I can go.** | คิดว่าไปได้ |
| | Khít wâa pai dâi. |

| **I can't come.** | มาไม่ได้ |
| | Maa mâi dâi. |

| **I can't go.** | ไปไม่ได้ |
| | Pai mâi dâi. |

| **I want to go.** | อยากไป |
| | Yàak pai. |

| **I want to go to Bangkok.** | อยากไปกรุงเทพฯ |
| | Yàak pai krung thêhp. |

While Bangkok (**baang kàwk**, place of the hog plums) is likely the old name of a village that existed before the establishment of the capital in 1782 by Rama I, Krungthep (City of Angels) is the name the Thais use for their capital.

| **I really want to go.** | อยากไปจริง ๆ |
| | Yàak pai cing cing. |

I don't want to go.   ไม่อยากไป
                                 Mâi yàak pai.

I really don't want to go.   ไม่อยากไปจริง ๆ
                                 Mâi yàak pai cing cing.

You went, didn't you?   คุณไปใช่ไหม
                                 Khun pai châi mái?

I went.   ไป
                                 Pai.

I didn't go.   ไม่ได้ไป
                                 Mâi dâi pai.

Don't go.   อย่าไป
                                 Yàa pai.

Don't go yet.   อย่าเพิ่งไป
                                 Yàa phôeng pai.

I must go now.   ต้องไปแล้ว
                                 Tâwng pai láeo.

May I go?   ไปได้ไหม
                                 Pai dâi mái?

May I go too?   ไปด้วยได้ไหม
                                 Pai dûai dâi mái?

Can we go?	เราไปได้ไหม Rao pai dâi mái?
Let's go.	ไป Pay. ไปเถอะ Pay thòe.

Thòe is a colloquial particle added to the end of sentences urging friends and co-workers. For example, "Let's go eat!" would be *Pai kin khâao kan thòe.*

Let's leave here.	ไปเถอะ Pay thòe.
Let's get out of here.	ออกไปจากที่นี่เถอะ Àwk pai càak thîi nîi thòe.
I'm leaving soon.	เดี๋ยวไป Dĭao pai.
She has left here.	เขาไปแล้ว Kháo pai láeo.
Stay here.	อยู่ที่นี่ Yùu thîi nîi.
Where are you going?	จะไปไหน Ca pai nǎi.

Please go first.

เชิญไปก่อน
Choen pai kàwn.

After you.

เชิญคุณก่อน
Choen khun kàwn.

Thanks for letting me go first.

ขอบคุณที่ให้ฉันไปก่อน
Khàwp khun thîi hâi
   chán pai kàwn.

Go slowly.

ไปช้า ๆ นะ
Pai chá cháa ná.

Go carefully.

ไปดี ๆ นะ
Pai di dii ná.

Like the verb/adverb *chaa* doubled to show "slowly in my opinion," the same goes for *di dii* where *dii* means good, and *di dii* becomes carefully, or well, in my opinion.

Eat, Drink, Be Merry!

6

I'm hungry.	หิว Hǐu.
I'd like to eat something.	ดิฉัน/ผมอยากกินอะไรหน่อย Dichán♀/Phǒm♂ yàak kin arai nàwi.
I haven't eaten yet.	ยังไม่ได้กินอะไรเลย Yang mâi dâi kin arai loei.
Do you want to eat?	คุณอยากกินไหม Khun yàak kin mái?
I don't want to eat.	ไม่อยากกิน Mâi yàak kin.
I'm full.	อิ่มแล้ว Ìm láeo.
I've finished already.	เสร็จแล้ว Sèt láeo. เรียบร้อย Rîap ráwi.
I won't eat.	ดิฉัน/ผมไม่กิน Dichán♀/Phǒm♂ mâi kin.

Did you eat (lunch/supper [dinner])?	คุณกินข้าว (กลางวัน/เย็น) แล้วหรือ Khun kin khâo (klaangwan/yen) láeo lŏeh?
What would you like?	จะกินอะไร Ca kin arai?
Do you want some more?	เอาอีกไหม Ao ìik mái?
I'm thirsty.	หิวน้ำ Hĭu náam.
I've got a dry throat.	ดิฉัน/ผมคอแห้ง Dichán♀/Phŏm♂ khaw hâehng.
I'd like to drink beer.	อยากกินเบียร์ Yàak kin bia.
Let's drink beer.	ไปกินเบียร์กัน Pai kin bia kan.
I don't want to drink.	ไม่อยากดื่ม Mâi yàak dùehm.

I won't drink.

ดิฉัน/ผมไม่ดื่ม
Dichán♀/Phŏm♂
mâi dùehm.

I haven't drunk yet.

ดิฉัน/ผมยังไม่ได้ดื่ม
Dichán♀/Phŏm♂ yang
mâi dâi dùehm.

Do you want to drink something?

คุณอยากดื่มอะไรไหม
Khun yàak dùehm
arai mái?

Do you want to drink some more?

คุณอยากดื่มอีกไหม
Khun yàak dùehm iik mái?

Thank you, but I still have some.

ขอบคุณ แต่ยังไม่หมด
Khàwp khun, tàe yang
mâi mòt.

Drink a little bit more.

ดื่มอีกหน่อยซิ
Dùehm iik nàwi sí.

Cheers! (formal)

ไชโย
Chai yoh!

Literally means "chink/crash glasses"

Cheers! (informal)

ชนแก้ว
Chon kâeo.

Have you ordered?

สั่งหรือยัง
Sàng rúe yang?

How about (some) dinner?

กินข้าวเย็นไหม
Kin khâo yen mái?

Is the meal ready?

อาหารเสร็จหรือยัง
Aahǎan sèt rúe yang?

It's ready.

เสร็จแล้ว
Sèt láeo.

Will you try this (food)?

ลองกินนี่ไหม
Lawng kin nîi mái?

Wanna taste?

ชิมหน่อยไหม
Chim nàwi mái?

(That) looks delicious.

น่ากิน
Nâa kin.

Smells good.

หอมจัง
Hǎwm cang.

Give me (some more).	ขออีกหน่อย Khǎw iik nàwi.
Enough.	พอ Phaw.
Enough?	พอไหม Phaw mái?
Not enough.	ไม่พอ Mâi phaw.
(Are you) **Full** (yet)?	อิ่มหรือยัง Ìm rúe yang?
Full.	อิ่มแล้ว Ìm láeo.
I can't eat that (I'm full).	กินไม่ไหว Kin mâi wǎi.
I can't eat that (it's yucky).	กินไม่ลง Kin mâi long.
Is this delicious?	นี่อร่อยไหม Nîi aràwi mái?
Delicious.	อร่อย Aràwi.

Very delicious.

อร่อยมาก
Aràwi mâak.

Not delicious.

ไม่อร่อย
Mâi aràwi.

Is this hot (spicy hot)?

เผ็ดไหม
Phèt mái?

Very hot.

เผ็ดมาก
Phèt mâak.

Not hot.

ไม่เผ็ด
Mâi phèt.

Please, not hot.

ขอไม่เผ็ดนะ
Khăw mâi phèt ná.

I don't like it.

ไม่ชอบ
Mâi châwp.

It's awful.

ไม่เอาไหน
Mâi ao năi.

(Tastes) Awful.

ใช้ไม่ได้
Chái mâi dâi.

What's that?

นั่นอะไร
Nân arai?

Not that.

ไม่ใช่อันนั้น
Mâi châi an nán.

What's this called?

นี่เรียกว่าอะไร
Nîi rîak wâa arai?

As You Like It 7

I like it.	ชอบ Châwp.
I like it a lot.	ชอบมาก Châwp mâak.
I appreciate (that)!	ดิฉัน/ผมอะพิเชต Dichán♀/Phŏm♂ ápichêht!*

* Derived from the English "appreciate."

I don't like it very much.	ไม่ค่อยชอบ Mâi khâwi châwp.
I hate it.	เกลียด Klìat.
I hate it a lot.	เกลียดมาก Klìat mâak.
I really hate it.	ดิฉัน/ผมเกลียดจริง ๆ Dichán♀/Phŏm♂ klìat cing cing.

I want that.	ดิฉัน/ผมอยากได้ ... Dichán♀/Phŏm♂ yàak dâi ...
I don't want that.	ดิฉัน/ผมไม่อยากได้ ... Dichán♀/Phŏm♂ mâi yàak dâi ...
I want to [verb].	อยาก ... Yàak [verb]

For instance, **yàak pai** means "I want to go."

I don't want to [verb].	ไม่อยาก ... Mâi yàak [verb]
I really don't want to [verb].	ไม่อยาก ... จริง ๆ Mâi yàak [verb] cing cing.
I'd like to [verb].	อยาก ... Yàak [verb]
I wouldn't like to [verb].	ไม่อยาก ... Mâi yàak [verb]

I'm busy.

ดิฉัน/ผมยุ่ง
Dichán♀/Phŏm♂ yûng.

Literally means "I've got work nuisance."

I'm happy.

ดิฉัน/ผมมีความสุข
Dichán♀/Phŏm♂ mii
  khwaam sùk.

I'm happy to hear that.

ดิฉัน/ผมดีใจที่ได้ยิน
Dichán♀/Phŏm♂ dii cai
  thîi dâiyin.

I'm sad.

ดิฉัน/ผมเสียใจ
Dichán♀/Phŏm♂ sĭa cai.

Cai literally means "heart" or "mind." It is an important word in Thai, and is often used as part of a compound to describe certain feelings which include:

  krehng cai, consideration for, or feeling of owing, someone
  plàehk cai, astonished, surprised
  dii cai, happy
  klûm cai, depressed
  phuum cai, proud
  tòk cai, shocked, scared
  cai ráwn, hot-headed
  cai yen, even-tempered

I'm fine.

สบายดี
Sabaai dii.

I'm angry.

โกรธ
Kròht.

I'm mad!

โมโห
Mohhŏh!

I'm mad at you!

โมโหคุณ
Mohhŏh khun!

I'm ready.

เสร็จแล้ว
Sèt láeo.

I'm tired.

(ดิฉัน/ผม) เหนื่อย
(Dichán♀/Phŏm♂) nùeai.

I'm freaked.

(ดิฉัน/ผม) ช็อค
(Dichán♀/Phŏm♂) cháwk.

I'm surprised!

แปลกใจ
Plàehk cai!

I'm sleepy.

(ดิฉัน/ผม) ง่วง
(Dichán♀/Phŏm♂) ngûang

I'm not sleepy.

(ดิฉัน/ผม) ไม่ง่วง
(Dichán♀/Phŏm♂)
    mâi ngûang.

I'm relieved (to hear that). โล่งอก
Lôhng òk

I'm scared. (ดิฉัน/ผม) กลัว
(Dichán♀/Phŏm♂) klua.

I feel sick. รู้สึกไม่สบาย
rúusùek mâi sabai.

I'm disappointed. (ดิฉัน/ผม) ผิดหวัง
(Dichán♀/Phŏm♂)
phìt wăng.

I was worried. (ดิฉัน/ผม) เป็นห่วง
(Dichán♀/Phŏm♂)
pen hùang.

I can do it. ดิฉัน/ผมทำได้
Dichán♀/Phŏm♂ tham dâi.

I can do it for you. ดิฉัน/ผมทำให้ได้
Dichán♀/Phŏm♂ tham
hâi dâi.

Can you do it? (คุณ) ทำได้ไหม
(Khun) tham dâi mái?

Can you do it for me? (คุณ) ทำให้หน่อยได้ไหม
(Khun) tham hâi nàwi
dâi mái?

I can't do it.	(ดิฉัน/ผม) ทำไม่ได้ (Dichán♀/Phŏm♂) tham mâi dâi.
Can't you do it?	(คุณ) ทำไม่ได้หรือ (Khun) tham mâi dâi lŏeh?
I can't help it.	(ดิฉัน/ผม) ช่วยไม่ได้ (Dichán♀/Phŏm♂) chûai mâi dâi.
Sorry, I can't.	ขอโทษ (ดิฉัน/ผม) ทำไม่ได้ Khăw thôht, (Dichán♀/ Phŏm♂) tham mâi dâi.
I should do it.	ดิฉัน/ผมควรทำ Dichán♀/Phŏm♂ khuan tham.
I shouldn't do it.	ดิฉัน/ผมไม่ควรทำ Dichán♀/Phŏm♂ mâi khuan tham.
I must do it.	ดิฉัน/ผมต้องทำ Dichán♀/Phŏm♂ tâwng tham.
I mustn't do it.	ดิฉัน/ผมต้องไม่ทำ Dichán♀/Phŏm♂ tâwng mâi tham.
I'll do it.	ดิฉัน/ผมจะทำ Dichán♀/Phŏm♂ ca tham.

I'll do it for you.	ดิฉัน/ผมจะทำให้ Dichán♀/Phŏm♂ ca tham hâi.
I'm tired of it.	(ดิฉัน/ผม) เบื่อ (Dichán♀/Phŏm♂) bùea.
I understand.	(ดิฉัน/ผม) เข้าใจแล้ว (Dichán♀/Phŏm♂) khâo cai láeo.
I understand very well.	(ดิฉัน/ผม) เข้าใจดี (Dichán♀/Phŏm♂) khâo cai dii.
I think I understand.	คิดว่าเข้าใจแล้ว Khít wâa khâo cai láeo.
I don't understand.	(ดิฉัน/ผม) ไม่เข้าใจ (Dichán♀/Phŏm♂) mâi khâo cai.
I don't understand very well.	(ดิฉัน/ผม) ไม่ค่อยเข้าใจ (Dichán♀/Phŏm♂) mâi khâwi khâo cai.
I know.	(ดิฉัน/ผม) รู้แล้ว (Dichán♀/Phŏm♂) rúu láeo.
I know him/her.	(ดิฉัน/ผม) รู้จักแล้ว (Dichán♀/Phŏm♂) rúucàk láeo.
I know that person.	(ดิฉัน/ผม) รู้จักคนนั้นแล้ว (Dichán♀/Phŏm♂) rúucàk khon nán láeo.

Do you know that?

รู้หรือเปล่า
Rúu rúe plào?

Ah, you know.

อ้อ คุณรู้
Âw khun rúu.

I don't know.

(ดิฉัน/ผม) ไม่รู้
(Dichán♀/Phŏm♂) mâi rúu.

I didn't know.

(ดิฉัน/ผม) ไม่เคยรู้
(Dichán♀/Phŏm♂)
   mâi khoei rúu.

**Give me time to
   think it over.**

ขอเวลาคิดดูก่อน
Khăw wehlaa khít duu
   kàwn.

I'll think about it.

(ดิฉัน/ผม) จะคิดดูก่อน
(Dichán♀/Phŏm♂)
   ca khít duu kàwn.

I'm confused.

(ดิฉัน/ผม) งง
(Dichán♀/Phŏm♂) ngong.

I'm so confused.

(ดิฉัน/ผม) งงมาก
(Dichán♀/Phŏm♂)
   ngong mâak.

I made a mistake.

(ดิฉัน/ผม) ทำผิด
(Dichán♀/Phŏm♂)
   tham phìt

I think I blew it.	คิดว่าทำเละไปหมดแล้ว Khít wâa tham lé pai mòt láeo.
I blew it.	ทำผิดไปแล้ว Tham phìt pai láeo.

I'm in a bad mood.	(ดิฉัน/ผม) กำลังอารมณ์ไม่ดี,
	อารมณ์เสีย
	(Dichán♀/Phŏm♂)
	  kamlang aarom mâi dii,
	  aarom sĭa.

Am I right?	(ดิฉัน/ผม) ถูกไหม (Dichán♀/Phŏm♂) thùuk mái?
Am I wrong?	ผิดหรือ Phìt lŏeh?

Sample Conversation 1: IN A JAM

SOMCHAI: **The traffic is crazy, isn't it?**	รถติดเป็นบ้าเลยนะ Rót tìt pen bâa loei ná?
FRANK: **Yes. Is it like this every day?**	ใช่ เป็นอย่างนี้ทุกวันไหม Châi, pen yàang níi thúk wan mái?

SOMCHAI: **You bet!**
You can have a traffic
jam at any time in
Bangkok.

ทุกวัน ในกรุงเทพฯ
รถติดตลอดเวลา
Thúk wan! Nai krung thêhp
    rót tìt talàwt wehlaa.

FRANK: **Oh no!**
We're going to be
late for our appointment.

ตายละเราจะไปไม่ทันนัดละซิ
Taai lá, rao ca pai mâi
    than nát lá sî.

SOMCHAI: **Be cool, Frank.**
Everyone understands
the traffic problem.

ใจเย็น ๆ แฟรงค์ ทุกคนรู้ว่ารถติด
Cai yen yen fráehng, thúk
    khon rúu wâa rót tìt.

FRANK: **There must be**
another way to
get around.

น่าจะมีทางอื่นไปได้
Nâa ca mii thaang ùehn
    pai dâi.

FRANK: **The traffic's**
hardly moved.
Maybe I should walk.

รถไม่ขยับเลย เดินไปดีกว่า
Rót mâi khayàp loehy,
    doehn pai dii kwàa.

SOMCHAI: **It's too**
far to walk.

ไกล เดินไม่ไหว
Klai, doehn mâi wăi.

FRANK: **What shall I do?**

ทำยังไงดี
Tham yang ngai dii?

SOMCHAI: **I've got it.**
  See that motorcycle
  taxi over there?
  (He points)
  Why don't you take
  one? It's faster/better.

รู้แล้ว เห็นมอเตอร์ไซค์
รับจ้างนั่นไหม ไปมอเตอร์ไซค์
เร็วกว่า
Rúu láeo, hěn mawtoehsai
  ráp câang nân mái?
  Pai mawtoehsai reo
  kwàa

FRANK: **Good idea.**
  (Gets out of car)
  I'm going, see you later.

ดี ไปก่อนนะ เจอกันใหม่
Dii, pai kàwn ná, coeh
  kan mài.

Sample Conversation 2: ON THE TOWN

DAO: **Let's sit over there.**

ไปนั่งที่นั่นกัน
Pai nâng thîi nân kan.

SIMON: **Don't you think**
  the table is too near
  the loud speakers?

โต๊ะนั้นใกล้ลำโพงไปไหม
Táw nán klâi lamphong
  pai mái?

DAO: **Hmm. How about**
  the table in the back?

ฮื่อ โต๊ะข้างหลังล่ะ
Hûeh, táw khâng lăng lâ?

SIMON: **Okay.**
  What do you want
  to drink?

ได้ (คุณ) จะดื่มอะไร
Dâi. (Khun) ca dùehm
  arai?

DAO: **Coke please.**

ขอโคล่า
Khăw khohlâa.

SIMON: **I'll order.**
  What music is playing
  tonight?

ผมสั่งให้ คืนนี้มีดนตรีอะไร
Phŏm sàng hâi. Khuehn níi
  mii dontrii arai?

DAO: **They have some Thai folk-rock singers I think you'll like a lot.**

มีเพลงเพื่อชีวิต คุณคงชอบมาก ๆ
Mii phlehng phûea chiiwít. Khun khong châwp mâak mâak.

Phleeng phûea chiiwít literally means "songs for life."

SIMON: **Great! So what's your favourite Thai folk-rock song?**

เยี่ยมเลยแล้ว เพลงอะไร คุณชอบมากที่สุด
Yîam loei, láeo phleng arai khun châwp mâak thîi sùt?

DAO: **I like "Made in Thailand" by Carabao.**

ฉันชอบ "เมดอินไทยแลนด์" ของคาราบาว
Chán châwp mehd in thailaen khǎwng khaaraabao.

SIMON: **I'll request it for you.**

เดี๋ยวจะขอให้
Dǐao ca khǎw hâi.

Mind Your Mouth!

Caution!!! Be especially careful about using the terms in this chapter, as they may cause offense.

What do you want?!	จะเอาอะไร
	Ca ao arai?!

Can be said to someone who is hassling you.

Do you want to say something?	จะบอกอะไรหรือ
	Ca bàwk arai lǒeh?
Don't stare at me!	อย่าจ้องอย่างนั้น
	Yàa câwng yàang nán!
What did you say?	อะไรนะ
	Arai ná?
Why do you talk like that?!	ทำไมพูดอย่างนั้น
	Thammai phûut yàang nán?!
You're stupid!	โง่
	Ngôh!
	ไอ้/อีโง่
	Âi/ii ngôh!

Âi (used when referring to males) and **ii** (used when referring to females) come from Isan (the NE region) and are part of the Lao language. When only one is indicated, this means that the phrase can only be directed towards one of the sexes. Lao (and Chinese) words are often used in slang and swear words. While these words are "everyday" words in Isan, they can cause offense when used inappropriately elsewhere.

You're stupid (and cheap)!

ขี้เง่า
Ngîi ngâo!

You look stupid!

ปัญญาอ่อน
Panyaa àwn!

That's stupid!

ไม่มีสมอง
Mâi mii samăwng!

Literally means "You've low intelligence."

What you did was stupid!

ทำโง่ ๆ
Tham ngôh ngôh!

You're crazy!

คุณประสาทขื่อบื้อ
Khun prasàat! sôehbôeh!

The next time someone cuts in front of your taxi and the taxi driver lets forth a stream of curses, you may hear a few of the following terms. Be **very** careful about using some of them yourself!

(You're) low class!

ชั้นต่ำ
Chán tàm!

(You're a) dog!!

ไอ้/อีหมาขี้เรื้อน
Âi/ii măa khîi rúean!!

Măa, a dog, is a strong insult. Dogs (especially muts) are considered the lowest of the animals and generally shouldn't be touched at all—besides they may be mangy or even rabid. You will, however, find pedigreed pets among more affluent Thais, and these can be treated as western-style pets.

Don't act stupid!

อย่าทำโง่ ๆ
Yàa tham ngôh ngôh!

Don't say stupid things!

อย่าคิดโง่ ๆ
Yàa khít ngôh ngôh!

You've got a big mouth!　ปากบอน
Pàak bawn!

Liar!　คนโกหก
Khon kohhòk!

That's a lie!　พูดโกหก
Phûut kohhòk!

Don't lie!　อย่าโกหก
Yàa kohhòk!

Stop it!　หยุดนะ
Yùt ná!

You shouldn't do that!　ไม่ควรทำ
Mâi khuan tham!

Why do you do such a thing?　ทำไมทำอย่างนั้น
Thammai tham yàang nán?

Leave him/her alone!　อย่าไปยุ่งกับเขา
Yàa pai yûng kàp kháo!

Don't bother him/her!　ปล่อยเขา
Plàwi kháo!*

* Literally means "Don't annoy/bother him/her!"

Do as I say!

ทำตามที่บอก
Tham taam thîi bàwk!

Back off!

ถอยไป
Thăwi pai!

This is the limit!

หยุดแค่นี้
Yùt khâeh níi!

Give it back!

เอาคืนมา
Ao khuehn maa!

Leave me alone!

ปล่อยฉัน
Plàwi chán!

Leave us alone!

อย่ายุ่งกับเรา
Yàa yûng kàp rao!

Get out of here!

ออกไป
Àwk pai!

Come here!

มานี่
Maa nîi!

You're noisy!

เสียงดัง
Sĭang dang!

Sit down and be quiet!

นั่งเงียบ ๆ
Nâng ngîap ngîap!

Shut up!

หุบปาก
Hùp pàak!

Stop your babbling!

หยุดพล่ามซะที
Yùt phlâam sá thii!

Be quiet!

เงียบ
Ngîap!

You asshole!

ไอ้/อีเหี้ย
Âi/ii hîa!!

Literally, *hîa* means "monitor lizard" and is, believe it or not, one of the worst things you can say to a Thai. AVOID this word if at all possible as it may cause extreme offense and even lead to a violent response.

You bitch!

อีแรด
Ii râet!

Râet means rhinoceros; it is not nice when directed at a woman.

You animal!

ไอ้/อีสัตว์
Âi/ii sàt!

You whore!

อีกะหรี่
Ii karìi!

Playboy!

ไอ้ขี้หลี
Âi khîi lǐi!

Shorty!

ไอ้เตี้ย
Âi tîa!

Weakling!

ไอ้เหี่ยว
Âi hìao!

You ain't got balls!

ไอ้หน้าตัวเมีย
Âi nâ tua mia!

You're ugly!

ไอ้น่าเกลียด
Âi nâa klìat!

You're pig!

ไอ้โสโครก
Âi sŏh khrôhk! *
ไอ้อ้วน
Âi ûan! **
ไอ้หัวล้าน
Âi hŭa láan! ***

* Literally means "dirty/filthy …"
** Literally means "obese …"
*** Literally means "… baldy"

Fag! Poof!

ไอ้กะเทย
Âi kathoei!

There are many terms for gays in Thailand, including **tòo** and **ii: àep**.

Tomboy!

ทอม
Thawm!

White boy!

ฝรั่ง
Faràng!
อั้งม้อ
Âng mâw! *

* From the Chinese Teochew dialect, often heard in Thailand.

ฝรั่งดอง
Faràng dawng! **

ไอ้หัวแดง
Âi hŭa daehng! ***

ไอ้ตาน้ำข้าว
Âi taa náam khâo! ****

* Literally means "pickled westerner"
** Literally means "red-haired..."
*** Literally means "rice water-eyed ..." (white-eyed)

A *faràng* is the general term for a westerner. It may have come from the Thai word for French people (*faràngsèht*), from Arabic (*farengi*), or it may go back as far as Sanskrit. Generally it is without pejorative connotations, but the other phrases may not be quite so neutral. Interestingly, *faràng* also means guava fruit. If children shout *faràng* at you, for fun you could reply *sapparót* (pineapple) or *mámûang* (mango)—this is bound to surprise!

You're the lowest!

ไอ้ถ่อย
Âi thàwi!

You're narrow-minded!

คนใจแคบ
Khon cai khâehp

Don't be so cocky!

ไอ้ขี้เก๊ก
Âi khîi kék!

Khîi used in front of other words shows a person's tendency toward doing or being something (both positive and negative). It appears in many compounds, including the following:

khîi lên, playful
khîi khui, talkative
khîi kìat, lazy
khîi mao, likes to drink heavily
khîi hûeng, jealous

You're a tightwad!
คนขี้เหนียว
Khîi nǐao!
ฝรั่งขี้นก
Faràng khîi nók! *

* *Faràng khîi nók*, literally "bird-shit westerner," is used to insult a
tourist who may not be stingy, but has little money to start with, eg a
backpacker travelling light, and so cannot show the expected "western"
extravagance. Note the similar word form to *phrík khîi nǔu*, literally
"mouse-shit chilli" because of its shape.

You're a dirtbag!
ไอ้สกปรก
Âi sòkkàbròk!

Get away!
ไปเลย
Pai loeh!
เย็ดแม่มึง
Yét mâeh mueng! *

* These mean "get lost", "get out of my sight" and "f...your mother."
Naturally they should be used with caution, especially the last one.

Serves you fucking right!
ช่างแม่มึง
Châng mâeh mueng!

Literally means "leave/let your mother go."

Go to hell!
ไปตกนรกซะไป
Pai tòk narók sá, pai!

Go play with yourself!
ไปชักว่าวซี่
Pai chák wâo sîi!

Literally means "go fly your kite," and is used only with men.

There's a line/queue here.
เข้าคิวซี่
Khâo khiu sîi

Don't push your way in!
อย่าแซงคิวซี่
Yàa saeng khiu sîi!

Don't push!

อย่าดัน
Yàa dan!

That hurts!

เจ็บนะ
Cèp ná!

Who do you think you are?!

ใหญ่มาจากไหนวะ
Yài maa càak năi wá?!

Damn it!

ปัดโธ่เว้ย
Pàt thôh wóei!

Shit!

โอ๊ย
Ói!

Lewd! (Vulgar!)

ไอ้ทะลึ่ง
Âi thalûeng!

Take your hand(s) off me!

เอามือออกไป
Ao mueh àwk pai!

Let me go!

ปล่อยนะ
Plàwi ná!

Don't touch me!

อย่ามาถูกตัวฉัน
Yàa maa thùuk tua chán!

I think you're trying to trick me!

จะหลอกฉันหรือ
Ca làwk chán lǒeh!

I think you're trying to cheat me!

ขี้โกงหรือเปล่า
Khîi kohng rúe plào!

Why is this so expensive?

ทำไมแพงนัก
Thammai phaehng nák!

Is it because I'm a westerner?

ราคาฝรั่งหรือเปล่า
Raakhaa faràng
rúe plào?

Literally means "Is this the price for *farangs*?"

Don't think I'm stupid!

ฉันไม่โง่นะ
Chán mâi ngôh ná!

I want to speak with the manager.

ขอพูดกับผู้จัดการหน่อย
Khǎw phûut kàp phûu càt
kaan nàwi

I'll tell all my friends!

จะบอกเพื่อน ๆ ให้หมด
Ca bàwk phûean phûean
hâi mòt!

I'll report you!

จะรายงานคุณ
Ca rai ngaan khun!

I'll tell the police!

จะแจ้งตำรวจ
Ca câehng tamrùat!

Hey! Tell me your name!

คุณ! ชื่ออะไร
Khun! Chûeh arai!

You better remember what you tried to do!

จำไว้นะว่าพยายามทำอะไร
Cam wái ná wâa
phayaayaam tham arai!

While Thais will try to avoid confrontations, bruised pride can bring about explosive results. Phrases like the two below may help defuse tension and get you out of a tight spot.

Take it easy!	ใจเย็น ๆ Cai yen yen!
Let's talk about it (the problem).	ค่อย ๆ พูดกัน Khâwi khâwi phûut kan.

Sometimes it's better to just accept blame (whether or not you are at fault) to defuse a threatening situation.

Okay, I'm wrong!	โอเค ดิฉัน/ผมผิดเอง Oh kheh dichán♀/phǒm♂ phìt ehng!
I'm sorry!	ขอโทษนะ Khǎw thôht ná

Okay, I accept it's my
  fault!
	โอเค ฉันยอมรับว่าฉันผิดเอง
	Oh kheh chán yawm ráp
	  wâa chán phìt ehng!

Steppin' Out 9

Are you having a good time?	สนุกไหม Sanùk mài?
Yeah, I'm having fun.	ดิฉัน/ผมกำลังสนุก Dichán♀/Phŏm♂ kamlang sanu-k.
We're having a good time aren't we?	เรากำลังสนุก ใช่ไหม Rao kamlang sanùk châi mái?
Did you two come here by yourselves?	คุณสองคนมากันเองหรือ Khun săwng khon maa ehng lŏeh?
Shall we drink together?	ดื่มด้วยกันไหม Dùehm dûay kan mái?
May I sit here?	ดิฉัน/ผมนั่งที่นี่ได้ไหม Dichán♀/Phŏm♂ nâng thîi nîi dâi mái?
Is someone sitting here?	มีใครนั่งหรือเปล่า Mii khrai nâng rúe plào?
Come over.	มานี่ซิ Maa nîi sî.
What's your name?	คุณชื่ออะไร Khun chûeh arai?

Guess what it is.	ทายซิ Thai sí.
It's a secret.	เป็นความลับ Pen khwaam láp.
Do you have a nickname?	มีชื่อเล่นไหม Mii chûeh lên mái?
Where do you live?	บ้านอยู่ที่ไหน Bâan yùu thîi năi?
Where do you come from?	มาจากไหน Maa càak năi?
How old are you?	อายุเท่าไหร่ Aayú thâorài?
Are you a student?	เป็นนักเรียนหรือเปล่า Pen nákrian rúe plào?
What do you do?	ทำงานอะไร Tham ngaan arai?
Where do you work?	ทำงานที่ไหน Tham ngaan thîi năi?
What do you do in your free time?	เวลาว่าง ทำอะไร Wehlaa wâang tham arai?
Do you come here often?	มาที่นี่บ่อยไหม Maa thîi nîi bàwi mái?
Have I seen you before?	เคยพบกันก่อนหรือเปล่า Khoei phóp kan kàwn rúe plào?

Your English is very good. พูดภาษาอังกฤษเก่ง
Phûut phaasăa angkrìt kèng.

What music do you like? ชอบดนตรีอะไร
Châwp dontrii arai?

Who do you like? ชอบใคร
Châwp khrai?

Do you know this song? รู้จักเพลงนี้ไหม
Rúucàk phlehng níi mái?

It's one of my favourites. เพลงโปรดของดิฉัน/ผม
Phlehng pròht khăwng dichán♀/phŏm♂.

I know [now]. อ๋อ รู้แล้ว
Ăw, rúu láeo.

I don't know. ไม่รู้
Mâi rúu.

Shall we dance? เต้นรำไหม
Tên ram mái?

I don't feel like dancing. ไม่อยากเต้น
Mâi yàak tên.

Let's talk a while. คุยกันก่อน
Khui kan kàwn.

You're a good dancer.	คุณเต้นเก่ง Khun tên kèng.
How did you hear about this place?	รู้จักที่นี่ได้ยังไง Rúucàk thîi nîi dâi yang ngai?

Rúucàk is to know someone, while *rúu* is to know something. The *càak* in the following line means "from."

I heard from my friends.	รู้จากเพื่อน Rúu càak phûean.
Where else do you go to dance?	คุณไปเต้นรำที่ไหนอีก Khun pai tên ram thîi năi ìik?
Where's that?	อยู่ที่ไหน Yùu thîi năi?
How long have you been in Thailand?	มาอยู่เมืองไทยนานเท่าไหร่แล้ว Maa yùu mueang thai naan thâorài láeo?
Were you born here?	เกิดที่นี่หรือ Kòeht thîi nîi lŏeh?
Do you like Thai girls?	ชอบสาวไทยไหม Châwp săo thai mái?
Do you like Thai guys?	ชอบหนุ่มไทยไหม Châwp nùm thai mái?
Like her/him. (pointing)	เหมือนเขา Mŭean kháo.
Hmm. He/She is lovely.	ฮึ่ม น่ารักดี Hûehm, nâa rák dii.

Let's party!
จัดงานกันดีกว่า
Càt ngaan kan dii kwàa!

Come and join us.
ไปเที่ยวกับเรานะ
Pai thîao kàp rao ná.

Come and have a good time with us!
ไปเที่ยวกับเราเถอะ
Pai thîao kàp rao thòe!

Let's get drunk!
เมากันดีกว่า
Mao kan dii kwàa!

What are you drinking?
คุณดื่มอะไร
Khun dùehm arai?

Have you been drinking a lot?
คุณดื่มกี่แก้วแล้ว
Khun dùehm kìi kâeo láeo?

Well, drink some more!
ดื่มอีกซิ
Dùehm ìik sîi!

You need to drink more!
คุณต้องดื่มอีก
Khun tâwng dùehm ìik!

You're a good drinker.
คอแข็งจัง
Khaw khăeng cang.

Literally means "You have a coppered throat."

Are you drunk?
เมาหรือ
Mao lŏeh?

Not yet.
ยัง
Yang.

I want more!
เอาอีก
Ao ìik!

Haven't you drunk too much?
ดื่มมากไปแล้วมั้ง
Dùehm mâak láeo máng?

Maybe you should stop drinking (now).
หยุดดื่มได้แล้ว
Yùt dùehm dâi láeo.

Are you okay?
โอเคหรือเปล่า
Oh kheh rúe plào?

You're kind.
คุณใจดี
Khun cai dii.

I like you.
ดิฉัน/ผมชอบคุณ
Dichán♀/Phŏm♂ châwp khun.

What time did you come here?
มาตั้งแต่เมื่อไหร่
Maa tâng tàeh mûearài?

What time is your curfew?
คุณต้องกลับบ้านกี่โมง
Khun tâwng klàp kìi mohng?

What time are you leaving?
จะกลับบ้านกี่โมง
Ca klàp bâan kìi mohng?

It depends.
แล้วแต่
Láeo tàeh.

If I have a good time, I'll stay.
ถ้าสนุกจะอยู่ต่อ
Thâa sanùk ca yùu tàw.

If it gets boring, I'll go (home).
ถ้าเบื่อก็กลับ
Yhâa bùea, kâw klàp.

What's next?
ต่อไปอะไร
Tàw pai arai?

Have you decided?	ตัดสินใจหรือยัง
	Tàtsĭn cai rúe yang?
Still thinking.	กำลังคิดอยู่
	Kamlang khít yùu.
No penny's dropping.	คิดไม่ออก
	Khít mâi àwk.
It's up to you.	แล้วแต่คุณ
	Láeo tàe khun.
Anything's fine.	ทุกอย่างเรียบร้อย
	Thúk yànng rîap ráwi.
Either will do.	อะไรก็ได้
	Arai kâw dâi.
I have a good idea.	คิดออกแล้ว
	Khít mâi àwk.
	ดิฉัน/ผมปิ๊งแล้ว
	Dichán♀/Phŏm♂ píng láeo. *

* Just like the ping of an idea!

Good idea.	แจ๋วมาก
	Căeo mâak.
	กุ๊ด ไอเดีย
	Kúdz aidia. *

Thai has no final d sound, so when a Thai tries to approximate it, the result is often halfway between an s and a z.

* From the English "good idea."

Good idea, low IQ.	ไอเดียสูง ไอคิวต่ำ
	Aidia sŭung, ay khiu tàm.

Said when you've made a dumb suggestion and your Thai friends make a little fun of you.

This is boring.
น่าเบื่อ
Nâa bùea.

Shall we leave?
ไปหรือยัง
Pai rúe yang?

Let's go.
ไปกันเถอะ
Pai kan thòe.

Shall we go somewhere else?
ไปที่อื่นกันไหม
Pai thîi ùehn kan mái?

Can my friends come?
เพื่อนดิฉัน/ผมไปด้วยได้ไหม
Phûean dichán♀/phǒm♂ pai dûai dâi mái?

I'd like to stay here longer.
อยากอยู่ต่ออีกหน่อย
Yàak yùu tàw ìik nàwi.

Anywhere's okay.
ที่ไหนก็ได้
Thîi nǎi kâw dâi.

There's a new place on ... Wanna go?
มีที่ใหม่ที่ ... อยากไปไหม
Mii thîi mài thîi ... yàak pai mái?

Sure.
ไปซี่
Pai sîi.

I'll take you home afterwards.
เลิกแล้วจะไปส่งบ้าน
Lôehk láeo ca pai sòng bâan.

I'll take you home.
เดี๋ยวจะไปส่งบ้าน
Dǐao ca pai sòng bâan.

| How does that sound to you? | คุณคิดว่ายังไง |
| | Khun khít wâa yang ngai? |

| I want to know more about you. | อยากรู้จักมากกว่านี้ |
| | Yàak rúucàk mâak kwàa níi. |

| Do you want to eat breakfast with me tomorrow? | อยากทานอาหารเช้าด้วยกันไหม พรุ่งนี้ |
| | Yàak thaan aahăan cháo dûai kan mái phrûng níi? |

| Do you want to stay the night? | อยากค้างไหม |
| | Yàak kháang mái? |

| Our thoughts are the same, right? | คิดตรงกัน ใช่ไหม |
| | Khít trong kan, châi mái? |

| Shall we meet again? | เราจะพบกันอีกไหม |
| | Rao ca phóp kan ìik mái? |

| When can I see you again? | จะพบกันอีกเมื่อไหร่ |
| | Ca phóp kan ìik mûearài? |

| May I call you? | โทร.ไปหาคุณได้ไหม |
| | Thoh pai hăa khun dâi mái? |

| May I have your phone number? | ขอเบอร์โทรศัพท์คุณได้ไหม |
| | Khăw boeh thohrasàp khun dâi mái? |

| Do you have a mobile phone? | มีมือถือไหม |
| | Mii mueh thŭeh mái? |

| Do you have something to write with? | มีกระดาษจดไหม |
| | Mii kradàat còt mái? |

I enjoyed myself today.	ดิฉัน/ผมสนุกมากวันนี้ Dichán♀/Phŏm♂ sanùk mâak wan níi.
I enjoyed myself tonight.	ดิฉัน/ผมสนุกมากคืนนี้ Dichán♀/Phŏm♂ sanùk mâak khuehn níi.
Take care.	ระวังตัวดี ๆ Rawang tua di dii.
See you later.	พบกันใหม่ Phóp kan mài.
See you tomorrow.	พบกันพรุ่งนี้ Phóp kan phrûng níi.

ON THE PHONE

May I speak to Miss/Mr... please?	ขอพูดกับคุณ ...หน่อยค่ะ/ครับ Khăw phûut kàp khun ... nàwi khâ♀/khráp♂
Which extension?	ต่อเบอร์อะไรคะ/ครับ Tàw boeh arai khâ♀/khráp♂
Please give me extension ... (number/name)	ขอต่อเบอร์ ... Khăw tàw boeh ... [number/name]
Hello, is this ...?	ฮัลโล นั่น ... หรือ Hallŏh nân ... lŏeh?
How are you?	สบายดีหรือ Sabai dii lŏeh.

I'm fine.
สบายดี
Sabai dii.

I've been waiting. Is there a problem?
ดิฉัน/ผมรออยู่ มีปัญหาหรือเปล่า
Dichán♀/Phŏm♂ raw yùu, mii panhăa rúe plào?

Yes, the traffic is terrible tonight.
ใช่ รถติดมากคืนนี้
Châi, rót tìt mâak khuehn níi.

Hold on please, I have another call.
รอเดี๋ยว มีสายเข้า
Raw dĭao, mii săi khâo.

The line was so busy.
สายไม่ว่างเลย
Săi mâi wâang loei.

I want to see you.
อยากเจอคุณ
Yàak coeh khun.

I want to see you now.
อยากเจอเดี๋ยวนี้
Yàak coeh dĭao níi.

Are you busy?
ยุ่งไหม
Yûng mái?

I'll call again later.
เดี๋ยวโทร.มาใหม่
Dĭao thoh maa mài.

I'll call tomorrow around six o'clock.
พรุ่งนี้จะโทร.มาตอนหกโมง
Phrûng níi ca thoh maa tawn hòk mong.

Please be home.
อยู่บ้านนะ
Yùu bâan ná.

What is your pager number?

เพจเจอร์เบอร์อะไร
Phehcôeh boeh arai?
โฟนลิงค์ แพกลิงค์เบอร์อะไร
Fohnlíng/pháeklíng *
    boeh arai?

* Phonelink and Pagelink are the names of pager companies. Company names can become absorbed into Thai in place of the item itself, e.g. *fáeb* for soap powder.

What is your mobile (phone) number?

มือถือเบอร์อะไร
Mueh tŭeh boeh arai?

Say hello to ... for me.

บอก ... คิดถึงนะ
Bàwk ... khít thŭeng ná.

LONELY TIMES

I'll miss you.

จะคิดถึงคุณ
Ca khít thŭeng khun.

I'll always think of you.

จะคิดถึงคุณเสมอ
Ca khít thŭeng khun
    samŏeh.

I'll always love you.

จะรักคุณเสมอ
Ca rák khun samŏeh.

I'll write you a letter.

จะจดหมายถึงคุณ
Ca còtmăi thŭeng khun.

Will you write to me?

จะเขียนถึงดิฉัน/ผมไหม
Ca khĭan thŭeng
    dichán♀/phŏm♂ mái.

I'll send you a postcard.
จะส่งโปสการ์ดมาให้
Ca sòng pohsàkàad
maa hâi.

I'll send you a nice photograph.
จะส่งรูปดี ๆ มาให้
Ca sòng rûup di dii
maa hâi.

I'll call you from America.
จะโทร.มาจากอเมริกา
Ca thoh maa láeo càak
amehríkaa.

I'll call you when I get to Australia.
ถึงออสเตรเลียจะโทร.มา
Thǔeng áwsatrehlia ca
thoh maa.

I'll call when I return.
กลับมาแล้วจะโทร.มา
Klàp maa láeo ca thoh
maa.

I'll be back soon.
จะกลับอีกไม่นาน
Ca klàp iik mâi naan.

Please understand.
เข้าใจนะ
Khâo cai ná.

I have to go because it's my job.
ต้องไปเพราะเป็นงาน
Tâwng pai phráw pen
ngaan.

Take care of yourself.
ระวังตัวให้ดี ๆ
Rawang tua hâi di dii.

Please wait for my return.
รอดิฉัน/ผมกลับนะ
Raw dichán♀/phǒm♂
klàp ná.

Don't cry.	อย่าร้องไห้ Yàa ráwng hâi.
Wipe your tears.	เช็ดน้ำตาซะ Chét nám taa sá.
I can't stand it!	ดิฉัน/ผมทนไม่ได้ Dichán♀/Phŏm♂ thon mâi dâi.
It's difficult for me, too.	ลำบากสำหรับดิฉัน/ผมด้วย Lambàak sămràp dichán♀/phŏm♂ dûai.
I miss you so much.	คิดถึงมาก Khít thŭeng mâak.

FILLER PHRASES

What a pity!	น่าเสียดาย Nâa sĭa dai!
Too bad.	ช่วยไม่ได้ Chûai mâi dâi.

Literally means "I can't help you."

I hope so.	คงยังงั้น Khong yang ngán.
It's risky.	เสี่ยง Sìang.
Go for it!	เอาเลย Ao loei!

Cheer up!

สดชื่นหน่อย
Sòt chûehn nàwi!

Calm down!

ใจเย็น ๆ
Cai yen yen!

Never mind.

ไม่เป็นไร
Mâi pen rai.

Original

แท้
Tháeh

Cool

เท่ห์
Thêh

Uncool

ไม่เท่ห์
Mâi thêh

Unbearable!

ดูไม่ได้
Duu mâi dâi!

Cute

น่ารัก
Nâa rák

Clever/smart

ฉลาด
Chalàat

Ugly

น่าเกลียด
Nâa klìat

Weird

แปลก
Plàehk

I can't believe (he/she/you) did that! (amused)

ไม่น่าเชื่อว่า ... ทำอย่างนั้น
Mâi nâa chûea wâa ...
tham yàang nán!

He/She/They is *kháo*, you is *thoe* (female only) or *khun*.

Lovers' Language 10

I'm crazy about you.
ดิฉัน/ผมหลงใหลในตัวคุณ
Dichán♀/Phŏm♂ lŏng nai tua khun.

I think I love you.
ดิฉัน/ผมว่า ดิฉัน/ผมรักคุณ
Dichán♀/Phŏm♂ wâa dichán♀/phŏm♂ rák khun.

I love you.
ดิฉัน/ผมรักคุณ
Dichán♀/Phŏm♂ rák khun.

I'm yours.
ดิฉัน/ผมเป็นของคุณ
Dichán♀/Phŏm♂ pen khăwng khun.

You're mine.
คุณเป็นของดิฉัน/ผม
Khun pen khăwng dichán♀/phŏm♂

Be mine.
เป็นของดิฉัน/ผมนะ
Pen khăwng dichán♀/phŏm♂ ná.

I want to know all about you.
ดิฉัน/ผมอยากรู้จักตัวคุณ
Dichán♀/Phŏm♂ yàak rúucàk tua khun.

Will you tell me?
จะบอกดิฉัน/ผมไหม
Ca bàwk dichán♀/phŏm♂ mái?

I'll tell you.

ดิฉัน/ผมจะบอกคุณ
Dichán♀/Phŏm♂ ca bàwk
   khun.

You look beautiful.

สวยจัง
Sŭai cang.

You're handsome.

หล่อจัง
Làw cang.

You're smart. (to a
  man only)

เท่ห์จัง
Thêh cang.

You're cute.

น่ารักจัง
Nâa rák cang.

You're sexy.

เซ็กซี่จัง
Séksîi cang!

Taxi!

แท็กซี่จัง
Tháeksîi cang!

Nearly rhymes with and means "sexy" here. Thais like to play with words
as much as or more than **_farangs_** do.

Look at me. (point)

ดูนี่
Duu nîi.

Let me see.

ไหนดูซิ
Năi duu sí.

I like your eyes.

ดิฉัน/ผมชอบตาคุณ
Dichán♀/Phŏm♂
   châwp taa khun.

You have beautiful eyes.

ตาคุณสวย
Taa khun sŭai.

I like it when you smile.
ดิฉัน/ผมชอบตอนคุณยิ้ม
Dichán♀/Phŏm♂ châwp tawn khun yím.

You have a beautiful smile.
คุณยิ้มสวย
Khun yím sŭai.
ยิ้มสวยจัง
Yím sŭai cang.

Flatterer!
ปากหวาน
Pàak wăan

Literally means "sweet mouthed"

You're quiet, aren't you.
วันนี้คุณไม่คุยเลย
Wan níi khun mâi khui loei.

Literally means "Today you're not chatty."

You smell sweet/nice.
หอมจัง
Hăwm cang.

May I kiss you?
ขอจูบหน่อย
Khăw cùup nàwi.
ขอหอมหน่อย
Khăw hăwm nàwi.

A western or *farang* kiss (*cùup*) is made with the lips.

Kiss me.

หอมดิฉัน/ผมซิ จูบผมซิ

Hăwm dichán♀/phŏm♂ sí

cùup dichán♀/phŏm♂ sí

A Thai kiss is more of a sniff (*hăwm*).

Where?

ที่ไหน

Thîi năi?

When?

ตอนไหน

Tawn năi?

เมื่อไหร่

Mûearài?

Can you stay with me tonight?

คืนนี้ค้างกับดิฉัน/ผมได้ไหม

Khuehn níi kháang kàp dichán♀/phŏm♂ dâi mái?

Can I stay with you tonight?

คืนนี้ค้างกับคุณได้ไหม

Khuehn níi kháang kàp khun dâi mái?

Can I sleep with you?

ดิฉัน/ผมนอนกับคุณได้ไหม

Dichán♀/Phŏm♂ nawn kàp khun dâi mái?

Do you want to eat breakfast together?

กินข้าวเช้าด้วยกันไหม

Kin khâo cháo dûai kan mái?

Don't be shy.

ไม่ต้องอาย

Mâi tâwng ai.

Close your eyes.	หลับตา Làp taa.
I'm embarrassed.	(ดิฉัน/ผม) เขิน (Dichán♀/Phŏm♂) khŏehn.
You look lovely.	น่ารักจัง Nâa rák cang.
You have a beautiful body.	รูปร่างคุณดี Rûup râang khun dii.
Will you look the other way for a second?	หันไปทางอื่นแป๊บหนึ่งได้ไหม Hăn pai thaang ùehn páep nùeng dâi mái?
Come a little closer.	เข้ามาใกล้ ๆ หน่อย Khâo maa klâi klâi nàwi.
Is this your first time?	นี่ครั้งแรกใช่ไหม Nîi khráng râehk châi mái?
Tell me the truth.	บอกความจริง Bàwk khwaam cing.
Don't worry.	ไม่ต้องกลัว Mâi tâwng klua.
Do you have a condom?	มีถุงยางไหม Khun mii thŭng yaang mái? มี "มีชัย" ไหม Mii "miichai" * mái? มีเสื้อฝนไหม Mii sûea fŏn mái? **

* The term (*miichai*) for a condom was adopted from the name of a
  former Cabinet minister, Khun Meechai Viravaydaya who popularised
  population control programs.

** Literally means "Do you have a raincoat?"

Please use a condom.	ใช้คอนดอมนะ Chái khawndawm ná.
I don't want to have a baby.	ไม่อยากมีลูก Mâi yàak mii lûuk.
We should have safe sex only.	เราควรใช้ถุงยาง Rao khuan chái thŭng yaang.

Literally means "We should use a condom."

I'm having my period.	ตอนนี้มีเม็น Tawn níi mii men.

Derived from English "menstruation."

We shouldn't do that, it's not safe.	ไม่ควรทำ ไม่ปลอดภัย Mâi khuan tham, mâi plàwt phai.
I understand.	ดิฉัน/ผมเข้าใจ Dichán♀/Phŏm♂ khâo cai.
Treat me kindly.	ทำเบา ๆ Tham bao bao.
Be gentle with me.	อย่ารุนแรง Yàa run raehng.
I really want you.	ดิฉัน/ผมต้องการคุณ Dichán♀/Phŏm♂ tâwng kaan khun.
Do you want me?	คุณต้องการฉัน/ผมไหม Khun tâwng kaan dichán♀/phŏm♂ mái?

It's been a long time.

ไม่ได้ทำมาตั้งนาน
Mâi dâi tham maa tâng naan.

Love me again.

เอาอีกที
Ao ìik thii.
ขอเบิ้ลนะ
Khăw bôen ná.

"To go again" is like asking for a "double" which gives the word *bôen*.

More and more.

เอาอีก เอาอีก
Ao ìik, ao ìik.

That's nice.

ดี
Dii.

That's very good.

ดีมาก
Dii mâak.

That's wonderful.

ชั้นหนึ่ง
Chán nùeng.

Literally means "first class."

That feels so good.

ดีจัง
Dii cang.

I feel so good.

สบายจัง
Sabai cang.

Touch me.

จับซิ
Càp sí.

Touch me there.

จับตรงนั้น
Càp trong nán.

Bite me.

กัดซิ
Kàt sí.

Stronger.

แรงหน่อย
Raehng nàwi.

A little softer.

เบาหน่อย
Bao nàwi.

Faster.

เร็วหน่อย
Reo nàwi.

Faster, faster.

เร็วเร็ว เร็วเร็ว
Reo reo, reo reo.

Slower.

ช้าหน่อย
Cháa nàwi.

Deeper.

ลึกหน่อย
Lúek nàwi.

Play (with me) more.

เล่นอีก
Lên ìik.

I can't hold back.

ทนไม่ไหวแล้ว
Thon mâi wǎi láeo.

I'm coming.

เกือบ (เสร็จ) แล้ว
Kùeap (sèt) láeo.

Did you like that?

ชอบไหม
Châwp mái.

Did you come?

เสร็จหรือเปล่า
Sèt rúe plào?

That was good.

ดีจัง
Dii cang.

That was sooo good.

ดีเหลือเกิน
Dii lǔea koehn.

That was wonderful.

เยี่ยมเลย
Yîam loei.

I don't want to leave you.

ไม่อยากไปเลย
Mâi yàak pai loei.

I want to stay with you.

อยากอยู่กับคุณ
Yàak yùu kàp khun.

Let's not get up yet.

อย่าเพิ่งลุกนะ
Yàa phôeng lúk ná.

**Let's stay together a
while longer.**

อยู่ด้วยกันอีกหน่อยนะ
Yùu dûai kan ìik nàwi ná.

**Let's stay in bed a little
longer.**

นอนต่ออีกหน่อยนะ
Nawn tàw ìik nàwi ná.

Let's have breakfast now.

ไปกินข้าวเช้ากันดีกว่า
Pai kin khâo cháo kan
dii kwàa.

The Other Side

11

I can't come here anymore.	มาอีกไม่ได้แล้ว Maa ìik mâi dâi láeo.
I can't see you anymore.	มาหาอีกไม่ได้แล้ว Maa hăa ìik mâi dâi láeo.
I won't call you anymore.	โทร.มาอีกไม่ได้แล้ว Thoh maa ìik mâi dâi láeo.
I like you, but I don't love you anymore.	ฉัน/ผมชอบคุณ แต่ไม่รักแล้ว Chán♀/Phŏm♂ châwp khun, tàeh mâi rák láeo.

When matters are less intimate, *chán* can be used instead of *dichán*.

I don't love you anymore.	ไม่รักอีกแล้ว Mâi rák ìik láeo.
I've stopped loving you.	ฉัน/ผมไม่รักคุณแล้ว Chán♀/Phŏm♂ mâi rák khun láeo.
You've stopped loving me.	คุณไม่รักฉัน/ผมแล้ว Khun mâi rák chán♀/phŏm♂ láeo.
I have another girlfriend/boyfriend.	ฉัน/ผมมีแฟนใหม่แล้ว Chán♀/Phŏm♂ mii faehn mài láeo.

Faehn comes from the English "fan."

I have someone else.
มีคนใหม่แล้ว
Mii khon mài láeo.

I love someone else.
รักคนอื่นแล้ว
Rák khon ùehn láeo.

I'm not interested in you anymore.
ไม่สนคุณอีกแล้ว
Mâi sǒn khun ìik láeo.

Being with you is no fun.
อยู่กับคุณไม่สนุก
Yùu kàp khun mâi sanùk.

You're boring!
น่าเบื่อ
Nâa bùea!

Stop bothering me!
อย่ากวน
Yàa kuan!

You don't love me anymore, do you?
คุณไม่รักฉัน/ผมแล้วใช่ไหม
Khun mâi rák chán♀/
phǒm♂ láeo châi mái?

Do you have another girlfriend/boyfriend?
คุณมีแฟนใหม่หรือเปล่า
Khun mii faehn mài rúe
plào?

Please tell me.
บอกหน่อย
Bàwk nàwi.

I want to know.
อยากรู้
Yàak rúu.

I'm sorry I haven't been a good girlfriend/boyfriend.
เสียใจนะ ฉัน/ผมไม่ได้เป็นแฟนที่ดี
Sǐa cai ná, chán♀/phǒm♂
mâi dâi pen faehn thîi
dii.

It's my fault.	ฉัน/ผมผิดเอง Chán♀/Phŏm♂ phìt ehng.
It's nobody's fault.	ไม่มีใครผิด Mâi mii khrai phìt.
These things happen.	มันเกิดขึ้นได้ Man kòeht khûen dâi.
Can we start again?	เริ่มใหม่ได้ไหม Rôehm mài dâi mái?
Should we try again?	ลองใหม่ดีไหม Lawng mài dâi mái?
I'm serious about you.	ฉัน/ผมจริงจังกับคุณนะ Chán♀/Phŏm♂ cing cang kàp khun ná.
I can't live without you.	ฉัน/ผมขาดคุณไม่ได้ Chán♀/Phŏm♂ khàat khun mâi dâi.
Please understand my feelings.	เข้าใจฉัน/ผมหน่อย Khâo cai chán♀/phŏm♂ nàwi.
I will never forget you.	จะไม่ลืมคุณเลย Ca mâi luehm khun loei.
Thanks for the beautiful memories.	ขอบคุณสำหรับความทรงจำที่ดี Khàwp khun sămràp khwaam song cam thîi dii.

Thanks for loving me.	ขอบคุณที่รักฉัน/ผม Khàwp khun thîi rák chán♀/phŏm♂
I'm so happy to have known you.	ดีใจที่รู้จักคุณ Dii cai thîi rák khun.
Remember me sometimes.	คิดถึงฉัน/ผมบ้างนะ Khít thŭeng chán♀/phŏm♂ bâang ná.
Will you think of me sometimes?	จะคิดถึงฉัน/ผมไหม Ca khít thŭeng chán♀/phŏm♂ mái?
Can we still be friends?	เรายังเป็นเพื่อนกันได้ไหม Rao yang pen phûean kan dâi mái?
Will you write to me?	จะเขียนถึงฉัน/ผมไหม Ca khĭan thŭeng chán♀/phŏm♂ mái?
Be happy with her/him.	ขอให้มีความสุขกับเขานะ Khăw hâi mii khwaam sùk kàp kháo ná.
I will always love you.	ฉัน/ผมจะรักคุณเสมอ Chán♀/Phŏm♂ ca rák khun samŏeh.